In and Out of Love:
Selected Poetry
from the 1970s

By Synthia
SAINT JAMES

Copyright 2015
Synthia
SAINT JAMES

I love hard

Make love softly

And hurt badly

If I could choose

Would I live with you

And not be resentful

For not fulfilling

My need

To live with me

To love

Or sign a contract

To love

May it be oral

Or written

I must love

Spontaneously today

Not sign a pledge

For tomorrow

My greatest fulfillment

As well as downfall

Is my ability of

Involvement

With others

I'm young now

Attractive, desirable

People pursue me

But one day soon

I'll be old

For age creeps up

On you

I realize it

Contend with it

But I must make

Something of myself

Leave my mark

Never to fade away

Never for people to

Look at me and say

What a beauty

She use to be

What a shame

But instead they'll

Look at my work

And say she's beautiful

My destiny hopefully

This will be

I learn more

About myself

Each and every day

A very sensitive

Person by nature

I strive and

Have strived

To strengthen myself

While at the same time

Balance myself

As much as possible

To remain sensitive

Within my strength

Today

Just another day

You never know

What exactly is in store

You go through

Another day

Filled with hopes

Promises

And even dreams

But living tomorrow

Can never be promised

So we must live

For today

Feelings

Have the power

To repeat themselves

Bury them as far

As you can

Deep within

But that certain

Someone

Can easily bring them

To the surface

Once again

When you smiled at me

I felt you

In the dark of

That crowded room

The rest of that night

And each day

Thereafter

My thoughts fell

Constantly on you

In just a little time

I was so happy to find

A glow had also

Started in you

I could call it love

It feels like love

Only time will tell

So I won't call it

Anything

Until I'm sure

I could make you feel

Like the one and only

I could cause you

To rely on me alone

But how selfish

That would be of me

I care about you

Much much more

I close my eyes

It's you I see

Smiling before me

The tenderest of smiles

Setting off a glow

Inside of me

I just talked to you

You sounded so good

So good, so good…

So often I feel

Proud of you

But I become

Lost for words

So please just know

I'm proud of you today

Tomorrow and even

Yesterday

To think of being

With you

Is to imagine being

Comfortable, loved

And lovable

Everyone has a place

In time

I hope that my place

Is beside you

Like an epidemic

You have spread

Into every fiber

Of this

My body

Your voice

The sweetest of

Sounds

To my ears

Your smile

The first taste of

Raindrops

For flowers on a

Hot bristly day

Your touch

A blanket covering me

With warmth

You to me

Have come to mean

So much

I've merged with you

You with me

Yet no change

Did it bring

To either of our souls

So beautifully

It has given

Us both more

Feeling you and

Things you need not

Say to me

I hear them

In your eyes

Feel them

In your touch

If I were a singer

I'd raise my voice high

And sing

A song for you

If I were a musician

I would compose

And play

The music for you

If I were a dancer

I would create a piece

And perform it for you

No matter where my

Talents may lay

I'd find

A very special way

To bring joy to you

This love of ours

Makes me happy

And it makes me sad

Happy

When you're glad

Sad when

You're feeling bad

One person's life

Depending

On another's

Two people

In love with each other

Feelings pop

Up to the surface

Given heat

And just a little time

In a strange

But tender way

You bring me

To the surface

You gnawed at my wall

Tore it down

Once again

Like always before

"Me" left unguarded

But surrounded

By your love

Love

You've brought

New meaning

Into my life

Once grey and cloudy

Now bright

And sunshiny

You've added beauty

To my every day

Minor things

Once big problems

My heart

Nearly shallow

I could have slept

My entire life away

Day breaks now

To find me wide awake

I can hardly wait

To start each new day

A day filled

With promise

Of happiness and

Of tomorrows

Beautiful days

I'm beginning to see

All the wondrous

Things around me

And to appreciate each

And every day

Love you've brought

New meaning

Into my life

You're a mystery to me

That I don't wish

To figure out

You're a part of me

It needs no explaining

I need you

For several things

Comfort, enjoyment

Creativity

And sometimes

Just to have someone

That I can laugh with

I feel warmed by you

You're a warm

Summer's night

I feel natural and

Easy with you

Once I'm there

Beside you

A unique attraction

A feeling of newness

My hope is for

Many dimensions

Of this I'm sure

Like a word

With added suffixes

Enables it to describe

You've given me

Something very special

That enhances

My creativity

Sitting here

Thinking of you

Feeling you

Thinking of me too

I love you

But not selfishly

But like the few

Who love you enough

To just want to see you

Happy

You're a cozy nest

I'm the captive bird

I love being

Enveloped by you

You're so warm

And I feel

At such ease inside

The love I feel for you

Makes me more loving

And free in the way

I love you

You compliment me

I you

That's hard to find

We're rare

Don't you agree

The day is coming

To a close

It's getting dark

Outside

But because of you

I feel nothing but light

Inside

I feel elated

Damn

If love isn't funny

One minute crying

The next

Laughing

I could talk with you

Hear your voice

Enjoy your presence

All day

Never get bored

Just greedy for more

Look into my eyes

And you'll see

Within me

Could you love

What you see

How do you

Tell someone

You love them

Make them believe

Its truth

Especially when

They don't even

Know you

The end of a love affair

The beginning

Of another

Either you fight

Becoming attached

Or you give it your all

You may end it quickly

Both ways

When I decided

Not to run again

I left myself wide open

To whatever comes

My way

And all the emotions

Direct outcomes

A big step

Oh yes

Could be scary

I guess

But it's a decision

I've got to stick with

Today I feel love

I'm a surging sea

My ocean welled up

Deep inside of me

When my time comes

I'll call my tides forth

My body then

Laid to rest on shore

When daybreak calls

My time to recede

Back I'll call my waters

Back inside of me

Here they'll await

The time

When again I'll release

This massive billow

Swelling inside of me

Today I feel loved

Love returned

Its energy

Creating intensity

Much like steam

Propelling a ship

Vapor causing mobility

Your love

Generates power

Gives me strength

Allows my love to exist

Today I feel love

Today I feel loved

Its power has

Overwhelmed me

To be with you

Makes me more aware

Of myself

And the things

Surrounding me

You inspire me

I look into your eyes

It may be just a picture

And I find hope, trust

And even desire

I feel faith in me

I have faith in you

Together we've got to

Work our way through

You encourage me

I you

Isn't it nice

To have someone

To lean on

Someone on your side

I'm on yours

I feel you on mine

Leaning back against

Feathery pillows

Cozy under warm

And fluffy blankets

Hearing the sounds

Of music

With you laying

Beside me

Watching TV

Or just talking

Simple things

That with you

I enjoy

Something about

Your touch

Starts a spark

That rages into

A three alarm fire

Wondrous sections

Of your body

By reactions

Let me know

Just where

I should place mine

Quivers, sighs

And moans

My mouth has given

My ears the pleasure

Of hearing

These sounds

From your lips

It's the quiet time

Of my night

I think of you

Visualize you

Feel you

Relive intimate times

Together

Hold those thoughts

And lull myself to sleep

Boy

Could I tear

Your body up

With many teeny

Tiny caresses

Strokes, nibbles

And sucks

Grips, my lips, tongue

And even my chin

Cover you

With every ounce

Of affection I have left

Then call

On my reserve

To prolong it yet

Waking to feel

The warmth of

Your body

Entwined with mine

Is worth waking up for

And wonderful

To fall to sleep by

Grey cloudy skies

Seeming ugly

Bring me

Memories of beauty

Beauty you gave to me

On just such a day

I love you

You'd have to be numb

Not to feel it

Blind not to see it

I give you

Whatever I can of me

Without not leaving

Enough of me

For me

What more could you

Be asking for

You've lost your

Initial excitement

That's expected

I guess

But with what's left

I can't help wondering

Will it carry us through

Sometimes you

Keep me waiting

Anxiously anticipating

A call

Or even a visit

Disappointments

I've felt

Anger withheld

With my feelings

Always crushed

Little things pile up

Jealousies flare up

Insecurity makes

Me believe

I'm losing you

I close myself off

You retaliate

Closing yourself off

The gap grows

I could have screamed

Last night

Declared my sorrow

And also my love

They were both

Called for

But nothing came forth

I felt on trial

A mother's child

Falsely accused

I hoped this feeling

Would take a recess

But today

I awoke

With it fresh

No moves will I make

Yours I'll await

I felt uneasy

Had nothing to say

Maybe tomorrow

This feeling

Will be swept away

Ego

Positive or negative

Our use

The determining factor

You have

Allowed yours

To become negative

It has caused me pain

But yours

Will be greater

You've placed

Too many obstacles

In your own way

But most of us learn

The hard way

I could have cried

But tears

Wouldn't have

Released me

Would only make me

Feel worse

So I picked up

My brush

And commenced

My work

I spoiled you

Therefore

I must have asked

For what I got

I cry

You cry

It's a release

That's all

A release

Sometimes I feel

Like a trophy

Awarded to the winner

Then placed on a shelf

To rest on a pedestal

I love hard

Make love softly

And hurt badly

www.ingramcontent.com/pod-product-compliance
Lightning Source LLC
Chambersburg PA
CBHW060200070426
42447CB00033B/2247